Who Is
Temple Grandin?

by Patricia Brennan Demuth

illustrated by Robert Squier

Penguin Workshop

Cheers to Joyce and Jack and their beloved
grandsons Caden and Tate Naylor;
and in memory of my dad, an early
champion of Temple's designs—PBD

For the students, families, and staff
of The Birchtree Center—RS

PENGUIN WORKSHOP
An Imprint of Penguin Random House LLC, New York

Visit us online at www.penguinrandomhouse.com.

Library of Congress Control Number: 2019038748

ISBN 9780451532510 (paperback)   10 9 8 7 6 5 4
ISBN 9780451532534 (library binding)   10 9 8 7 6 5 4 3 2 1

Contents

Who Is Temple Grandin?

"Weirdo."

"Oddball."

Once again, the kids were tossing insults at Temple Grandin in the hallway of junior high school.

They picked on Temple because she didn't act like everybody else. She spoke in a loud, flat voice. She repeated sentences over and over, word for word. She clapped her hands over her ears at the sound of the school bell. She acted lost and afraid in the crowded school hall.

Kids couldn't understand what made Temple tick. And Temple couldn't understand them, either. That was because Temple's brain worked differently from theirs. She had been born with a developmental disorder known as autism (say: AW-tiz-im). It showed up when she was a baby, making her behave in odd ways.

On this day, Temple's temper boiled over at the bullying. She hurled a book at a kid. Hours later, the principal expelled her from school. Probably no one was too surprised. Temple was flunking nearly all her subjects. They just didn't interest her.

Everyone back in 1961 would have been amazed to know that Temple would grow up to become a world-famous animal scientist. All through her career she has worked to improve the treatment of cows and other animals that are raised for food.

Every year, millions and millions of cattle are killed for beef. Until Temple came along, people thought of cattle as products to turn into hamburgers and steaks. But Temple paid attention to the fear and pain cattle felt at large meat plants.

As an autistic person, Temple often felt like

a scared animal herself. Loud noises, unfamiliar objects, sudden movements—any of those might frighten her at any minute. Her fears helped Temple tune in to the way animals feel.

What Is It Like to Have Autism?

Autism is a disorder that affects the way a person behaves. The disorder affects people in a wide range of ways. On one end are children who never learn to speak and are locked inside their own world. At the other end are children who have some quirks but grow up to lead successful, independent lives.

Many children with autism

- have a hard time understanding other people's feelings
- have trouble with speech
- often repeat words and certain actions again and again
- are highly sensitive to loud noises, bright lights, strong smells, and rough fabrics
- are very good at some things and very poor at others
- tend to "space out" and block out the outside world
- become obsessed with certain interests and projects (for example, trains or computers)
- dislike change to their routine

Little by little, she changed the meat industry. Thanks to Temple, people began to realize that cattle are creatures with feelings that deserve a good life to the end.

Does autism make Temple more aware of animals' feelings? Temple thinks so. It makes her accept herself just the way she is. She has said many times, "If I could snap my fingers and be non-autistic, I would not. Autism is part of who I am."

CHAPTER 1
An Unusual Child

Mary Temple Grandin was born in Boston in 1947. Her family called her by her middle name, Temple. To this day, that's how everyone knows her.

Her parents, Eustacia and Richard, were educated and well-to-do. Nothing unusual set the Grandins apart from other couples. But their firstborn child wasn't at all like other children.

Other babies cuddled up to their mothers. But when Eustacia hugged Temple, her child clawed at her like a wild animal. Other babies smiled and cooed and laughed. Not Temple. Later, when Temple did laugh, her mother said, "It erupts out of her in uncontrollable spasms, along with spitting."

Youngsters usually start talking around age two. Temple never spoke a word. Instead she screamed, hummed, and made peeping sounds while flapping her hands.

And she was destructive. Temple broke her toys and ripped wallpaper off the wall. She chewed puzzle pieces and spat out the mush. In wild temper tantrums, she yanked off her shoes and threw them—hard.

Of course other toddlers threw tantrums, too. But Temple's were longer, louder, and more furious. There were days when Temple seemed fine. Then suddenly, she'd throw herself on the floor, kicking and screaming.

Eustacia was only nineteen when Temple was born. She worried that she was doing something wrong with her daughter. She wasn't. A second daughter, Jean, born when Temple was almost two, behaved just fine. In all, the Grandins had four children—three daughters and a son. None of the other children acted like Temple.

Between fits, Temple spaced out, locked inside her own world. For hours on end, she rocked back and forth on the floor, gazing at the rug. She spun lids and coins endlessly. When Temple zoned out, she blocked all sounds, even her mother's voice calling her name. It seemed as if headphones covered her ears.

Was Temple deaf, her mother wondered?

Richard didn't think so. He thought Temple belonged in a hospital for children with mental problems. Most people at that time agreed with him, even doctors. Very little was known about autism in the 1940s. Children like Temple usually spent their lives in hospitals, away from their families and the real world. Eustacia couldn't bear the thought of that. Later, Temple became deeply grateful to her mother for not giving up on her.

In 1950, when Temple was three, Eustacia brought her to a neurologist, a brain doctor. Tests proved that Temple was not deaf. Her intelligence was normal, too. (Later tests showed Temple was extremely smart.) The doctor suggested speech therapy. Maybe Temple could be taught to talk.

Speech therapy became a huge breakthrough in Temple's life. Until then, words had sounded like a jumble of unclear sounds to her. She heard only parts of words. For example, she heard "ba" instead of "ball." The speech teacher pronounced every word very slowly so Temple could hear the missing sounds and say them herself.

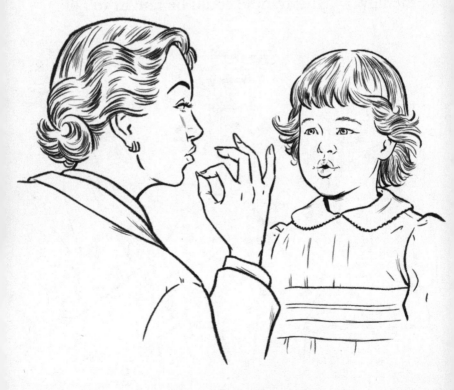

Bit by bit, a light turned on in Temple's brain. She was a bright child with a mind that longed to break free. After a while, she forced out single words. By the time she was five, Temple talked in sentences. From then on, she turned into a jabber box. She talked nonstop.

A nanny also helped Temple behave in a group. Temple learned simple manners and how to take turns at games. By then, Temple didn't want to be shut out of family games, even if she wasn't sure how to play like the others.

Still, her terrible tantrums and zoning out continued. So, when Temple was five, her mother brought her to a psychiatrist. For the first time, Eustacia learned the word that described what was happening: *autism*.

Because of autism, Temple's senses were supercharged. Ordinary sights, smells, and touches were a nightmare to Temple. The jangle of a ringing telephone hurt her ears. The strong smell of a rose drove her crazy. Starched dresses felt prickly against her skin. When her senses were overloaded, Temple lashed out in tantrums.

One time when she was three, Temple nearly caused a terrible car accident because of a scratchy hat. Eustacia was driving Temple to speech therapy down a busy highway. In the back seat, Temple tore off a hat that her mother had made her wear. It felt prickly and painful.

Leaning forward, Temple threw it out her mother's open window. Eustacia tried to grab the hat—and sideswiped a big truck! It was extremely fortunate that no one was hurt.

The real world was often a confusing place to Temple. But, at five, she was at the age to start school. Was Temple ready to take this big step?

CHAPTER 2
Grade School Years

Luckily, Temple's grade school was right down the road from where they lived in a big house. If Temple exploded in a tantrum at school, Eustacia could get there fast and bring her home.

It was also lucky that Dedham Country Day School was small and private. There were only fourteen children in Temple's class. All the families knew one another. Every child was invited to every birthday party. No one was ever left out— and Temple wouldn't be, either.

When Temple walked into the classroom on the first day, the kids didn't see anything unusual—just a tall girl with short brown hair. But before long, Temple's unusual behavior showed up. She always called her classmates by their first *and* last names. Her voice was loud and flat, and her speech was slurred. Temple repeated the same questions

over and over again, just to hear the same answers. And sometimes she completely lost it.

During one meltdown, Temple threw herself on the floor, kicking and screaming. When the teacher came over to calm her, Temple bit her on the leg! Her classmates looked on with shock.

No one could see inside Temple's brain to understand what made her explode. Children with autism need a steady routine. Maybe there had been too many changes in the schedule for Temple that day. Maybe the smell of the teacher's perfume was too strong for her to bear. Maybe the school bell rang one too many times. Temple has said that the clanging school bell felt like a dentist drill hitting a nerve.

Temple didn't know that she was different from other children. She thought the school bell hurt them, too. "I thought other people could

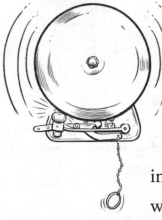

withstand the noise because they were stronger than me," she later recalled.

Sure, Temple acted differently. But like every child, she wanted badly to fit in. Being left out or made fun of was another reason to explode.

One day in music class, Temple couldn't clap to the beat, although she didn't realize it. "Why are you acting this way?" the teacher asked her. "You're spoiling it for everyone." Temple was hurt. She had been trying with all her might. Furious, she jumped up, knocking over her chair.

Temple flinched like a scared animal at the slightest touch, even the teacher's tap on her shoulder. Secretly, though, Temple longed to be hugged. To comfort herself at home, Temple wrapped herself tightly in a blanket or wiggled under couch cushions. In class, she daydreamed about a magic box that could wrap her tightly in a hug. Who could imagine that one day Temple would invent her own "magic" hugging box?

For all her problems, Temple had amazing talents, too. In art class, she drew beautiful lifelike drawings of horses. And she could invent and build things herself. Her skilled hands made sailboats, tree houses, and kites shaped like animals that she flew with her sisters and brother.

She sewed costumes for school plays on a little sewing machine her mother gave her.

At home, in her room, Temple rigged up webs of strings that dropped over "invaders"—that meant anyone who came in without being asked.

Curious neighborhood children trooped along with Temple on her after-school projects. One of her young pals said she liked being with Temple because she wasn't ever boring.

Sometimes Temple's active mind thought up mischief. It was fun for her, but dangerous for others. One day, she and a friend threw bottles out of the hayloft of an old barn. The teacher lived next door, and the bottles shattered all over the teacher's yard. The next day, Temple blamed

the mess on two boys who sometimes made fun of her. Today, Temple knows that's wrong. But at the time, she thought it served the bullies right.

For the most part, grade school was a happy time for Temple. But, at the end of sixth grade, it was time for Temple to start junior high school. It would turn her world upside down.

CHAPTER 3
Teasing and Torment

The Cherry Hill Girls School, the junior high that Temple attended in 1960, was so different from the quiet pace of her grade school. There were thirty to forty girls in the seventh grade and hundreds in the school. Class sizes were large.

All day long, students moved from one classroom to another, with a different teacher for each subject. The jammed hallways buzzed with noise and motion. Locker doors slammed. Kids talked, laughed, and shouted out to their friends. Temple had to get used to something new all the time. And that was so hard for her.

The very worst part of junior high was

having kids poke fun at her. Dedham Country Day School had been like a big family. For the most part, her classmates had accepted Temple. But now, mean students called her names. They mocked the way she repeated words, calling her the "oddball tape recorder." The hallways and the lunchroom became dreaded danger zones for Temple.

Did the kids think that their cruel jabs didn't bother Temple? If so, they were very wrong. Everything about Temple was intense—including her deep emotions. To this day, Temple recalls the "total torture" of being bullied. "I just wanted the kids to stop teasing me," she recalled in a film about her life. "That's all I could think about. And that's miserable, let me tell you."

Temple's grade school classmates had enjoyed her creative projects. But the girls, older now, were interested in fashion, popular music, and—especially—boys. Temple could not care less about these things. She didn't understand the girls any more than they understood her. Her autism prevented her from "reading" their faces. When the girls rolled their eyes, Temple didn't realize they were bored or put off. (In fact, she was fifty before she learned the meaning of an eye roll.)

Jokes and sarcastic remarks also went right

over her head. Temple didn't understand that sometimes words spoken in a certain way meant the opposite of what they normally did (like saying "Yeah, *right*!" when you mean "No way!"). She always said exactly what she meant and just assumed that others did, too.

In class, Temple spent her time dreaming up clever pranks to get back at classmates. Once, she rigged the cords of the window blinds to a student's desk. When the student opened the desk—*CRASH!*—the blinds slammed down. Temple chuckled to herself. The kids may have thought she was weird, but she was showing them that she sure wasn't stupid!

One day, Temple just couldn't take any more of the insults. In the hallway between classes, a girl called her a mean name. Furious, Temple hurled a book at the girl's face, hitting her in the eye. Without a glance back, Temple stalked off.

That night, the phone rang while the Grandins relaxed in the living room. Temple went to answer it. The caller was the school principal. He said she wasn't allowed back at school. She was expelled!

Pale and upset, Temple returned to the family and told her parents what had just happened.

Richard Grandin became furious at Temple. Eustacia quietly took another approach. She began getting information on other schools, hoping she could find someplace where Temple could fit in and be happy.

CHAPTER 4
School Away from Home

Fourteen-year-old Temple and her mother drove up a dirt road, high into the forested mountains of New Hampshire. Finally, they reached this sign next to a gravel driveway:

Hampshire Country School

Student Population—32

Elevation—1,000 feet

Here was the small boarding school where Temple would spend her high-school years. (At a boarding school, students live on the campus during the school year.)

Hampshire Country School had been founded for kids like Temple. All were bright, talented kids who had trouble fitting in elsewhere. Not all of them had autism. Great importance was placed on students getting along together and taking responsibility for their actions.

Besides the classroom buildings, there was a working farm on campus that the students helped run. Horses, sheep, and cows grazed in the fields. Barns and sheds dotted the property. The school was located on 1,700 acres of wooded mountain land, filled with ponds, streams, and old stone walls.

Eustacia Grandin helped Temple move into the top floor of a dorm that once had been a big old farmhouse. Then it was time for her to say goodbye. Away from home for the first time, Temple longed for a hug. But her autism kept her rigid as a board. She still couldn't let her mother touch her.

That night at dinner, Temple got off to a rocky start. A girl cut into the food line in front of her. Temple hit her. Miss Downey, a teacher who had witnessed the scene, quietly led Temple away to a table. She first let Temple know that she understood her reason for being upset. Then she firmly added that, no matter what, hitting was never allowed. Miss Downey's fairness made Temple feel better. But kind words alone were not going to stop Temple from using her fists to settle problems. What helped her do that were horses.

Temple immediately took to the nine horses that lived in the school's stable. She spent every spare minute in the stables—pitching hay, grooming the horses, and cleaning the stalls. Temple's classes didn't interest her the way horses did. She could calm them while a blacksmith fitted their hooves with metal shoes. And she became a superb rider.

A very wild-eyed, hot-tempered horse named Bay Lady was Temple's favorite. Her classmates marveled that Temple could ride her. Nobody else could.

Horses are excitable animals who may balk easily at anything out of place. Autism helped Temple to notice things other people didn't. So right away she understood Bay Lady's nervous signals. The horse's ears pricked up in anger. When afraid, Bay Lady swished her tail, faster and faster. Temple adjusted her riding so Lady was never scared or nervous.

Temple understood what Bay Lady was feeling so much more easily than she could figure out people.

The horses became Temple's new passion. But, after six months at Hampshire Country School, her outbursts of temper hadn't stopped.

One afternoon, Temple smacked a classmate who laughed at her when she tripped on a croquet wicket. The ever-patient Miss Downey had reached her limit. This time, she didn't let Temple go riding for a week.

Seven days without her beloved horses! It seemed like forever to Temple. She never wanted to be punished like this again. So she made up her mind to stop hitting. And she did—for good.

Emotions still boiled up inside Temple. Instead of lashing out, Temple now released them by crying. She ran to someplace private and sobbed until she calmed down.

During high school, Temple got better and better at inventing and building things. Temple thought in pictures, not words. In her mind, she could see each part of something that she was building. Then she put the parts together and turned the invention all the way around in her mind. Today, Temple compares it to running a movie in her head.

Mr. Davis, the ski teacher, designed a rope tow up a nearby ski slope. Now classmates didn't have to lug all their gear and skis up the seventy-foot climb. Ever handy with tools, Temple also put tongue-and-groove wood siding on the ski tow

house, put shingles on the horse-barn roof, and helped carpenters remodel a house.

Temple made friends and took part in school outings. Yet, autism still set her apart. Temple was clueless about why other girls fussed over their hair and makeup. What made them get wild crushes on rock stars? And why did her roommate fall to the floor screaming when the Beatles came on TV?

A posed school picture in 1965 shows the girls in Temple's class dressed up in ironed blouses and wearing hair bows. Temple stands at one end, tall and serious, dressed in the same jacket she wore day in and day out. She didn't like change—not even for picture day.

Hampshire Country School

Hampshire Country School was founded in 1948 by Henry Patey, a psychologist, and Adelaide Patey, a teacher. They enrolled a small number of bright, intense boys and girls who had trouble adjusting in bigger school settings. Their school provided a safe place for kids to develop their unusual, sometimes quirky, interests.

CHAPTER 5
The Squeeze Machine

During high school at Hampshire Country, Temple's new self-control faced a threat. She was growing into a young woman. Changes in her body upset her entire nervous system. She began to have frequent panic attacks.

The panic attacks made Temple's heart race and pound. Her palms got sweaty. Her hands and legs trembled. It felt like a huge lump was in her throat that made it hard to swallow or breathe.

Attacks could be set off by anything, anywhere. As always, sudden sounds, as well as smells and touches, alarmed her. A ringing phone filled her with dread. What if the phone call were to tell her bad news? Temple started to avoid class outings. She was scared of being in public when an attack

hit. And there was nothing Temple could do to stop the attacks.

Or could she?

At fifteen, Temple was about to discover a surprising solution. She spent summer vacation at the ranch owned by her Aunt Ann in Arizona. Her usual fear of being in a new place vanished right away. Temple fell in love with ranch life and the wide-open spaces of the West. (Today, she still lives out west, in Colorado.)

Every day was filled with hard chores, and Temple pitched right in. In no time flat, she was a terrific ranch hand, mending fences and rebuilding a roof.

Temple's amazing skills as an inventor also made life easier for Aunt Ann. Temple had noticed her aunt had to get out of the truck to open the big ranch gate. Then, after driving through, Aunt Ann had to walk back and push the gate closed again. So Temple figured out a new system. It let her aunt open the gate from the driver's seat by pulling a rope. The gate would automatically close after the car passed through.

That summer, Temple grew fond of cattle. She'd never really been around them before. In pastures, the huge beasts were peaceful, curious animals.

One sunny afternoon, Temple stood with Aunt Ann watching the vet give shots to the cattle. A machine called a cattle chute held each steer in place so it wouldn't lash out and get hurt or hurt any of the people nearby. A hole in front of the wooden chute held the cow's head in place. The sides of the chute pressed inward against the cow's body.

Cattle chute

Temple saw that the cattle were nervous until the sides of the chute closed around their bellies. Right away the cattle calmed down.

Temple wanted to try it herself! When the vet and cowboys had herded the cattle away, Temple asked her aunt to close her inside the chute.

It was a strange request. But Aunt Ann kept an open mind. Temple placed her head inside the opening; Aunt Ann pulled the ropes that closed the sides.

Peace swept over Temple. She relaxed in the chute for a half hour. Afterward, she felt calm for a long while. Temple had stumbled upon a way to soothe herself. It was the answer to her anxiety attacks.

Temple began relaxing inside the cattle chute every day. It felt like getting the hugs she'd always ached for. Only now she could get hugged on her own terms without feeling overwhelmed.

As vacation came to an end, Temple couldn't bear the thought of leaving the relaxing cattle chute behind. Of course, Temple couldn't lug it all the way to New Hampshire. So, back at school, she hammered together her own model out of plywood. Temple called it the Squeeze Machine. It fit in her dorm room. Every day, she asked her roommate to close her inside so her nerves could unwind. (Later, Temple added an air compressor to the machine so she could close and open the sides herself.)

A cattle chute in the dorm was too weird for some of the staff. The school counselor mocked Temple's strange new contraption. But the science teacher, William Carlock, came to Temple's aid.

He suggested she use science to test out her machine. By doing research, maybe she could show that a cattle chute made people relax, too.

Temple tackled the project with gusto. She asked classmates to try out the Squeeze Machine. Like a research scientist, Temple stood by with a clipboard and recorded their reactions. Some kids didn't like the Squeeze Machine, but many reported it was relaxing.

The Hug Machine

Versions of Temple's squeeze machine are now sold worldwide. It's often called a "hug machine" or "hug box." Studies proved that it lowers blood pressure and heart rate and helps autistic people relax deeply. Today's models are far more advanced than Temple's early one. Padded side cushions can be automatically adjusted by controls held in the user's hands.

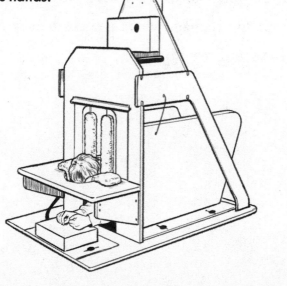

Temple got to keep her machine. There is now a published scientific paper about her research.

Science quickly became Temple's passion. It gave her a high goal: to attend college and become a real scientist. Classes had always been boring, boring, boring. But not anymore. Ds and Fs on her report card changed to As.

The rough years of high school were behind her. Temple had overcome her terrible temper outbursts and panic attacks. In a book she wrote later, Temple said, "Animals saved me. I got through my teenage years thanks to my Squeeze Machine and my horses."

CHAPTER 6
A New Career

At one time, people didn't expect Temple to finish grade school. Yet in 1970, she graduated second in her class from Franklin Pierce College.

Then she went on to graduate school at Arizona State University. Later, she would get her PhD, the highest possible university degree!

Her interest was animal science. Temple wanted to study how cattle behaved in different

kinds of chutes. Did certain squeeze machines work better than others?

But here was the hitch: There weren't any school programs like that. Not at Arizona State University or anywhere else. The usual livestock studies in the 1970s dealt with animal feeding, breeding, and medicine. (Livestock are large animals raised for meat, such as cattle and hogs.) Scientists certainly never focused on how animals felt. And they never considered that ordinary farm equipment could affect animal behavior or health.

That didn't stop Temple. She marched across campus to the departments of construction and industrial design. There she found professors willing to help her study how farm equipment affected animal herds. Without realizing it, Temple was starting a brand-new field of study. (Today, university programs like it are widespread—and they use textbooks written by Temple!)

Her studies led Temple to feedlots throughout Arizona. A feedlot is where farmers send their cattle to fatten up on grain before they are killed.

Temple watched every move of the cows and their handlers. She scribbled detailed notes about how the cows behaved in different chutes. Temple published her unusual findings in a magazine called *Arizona Farmer Ranchman.*

Cattlemen who had worked with cattle all their lives taught Temple a lot. Many of them knew just how to handle the animals. But Temple also saw men mistreat the cattle. This hurt the animals' health. Stressed cattle grew slowly and got sick more often.

Seeing cattle mishandled upset Temple deeply. "I can put myself into a steer's 1,200-pound body and *feel* the equipment," she has written. "When I see someone squeeze an animal too hard in a squeeze chute, it makes me hurt all over."

Temple decided to make the welfare of livestock her life's work. How? By designing equipment that kept the huge beasts safe and comfortable.

Cattlemen in the livestock business didn't welcome Temple. Back then, the meat industry was a man's world. Lots of guys resented a woman hanging around, especially one who inspected how they did things. They tried to get rid of her. Once, a cowboy foreman at a feedlot put bull testicles on her car. Temple simply wiped the mess away.

Another day a burly man named Ron blocked Temple's way into a feedlot. He stood in front of the door with his legs wide apart and growled that no woman could go inside.

Temple's stubborn streak flared. No one was going to stop her work. Then a brainstorm hit her. If she could get a press pass, she could enter any feedlot in Arizona. Temple drove to the offices of *Arizona Farmer Ranchman*, the magazine that had been publishing her articles. She asked to write a column for the magazine that would appear every month. Her interesting articles quickly became a hit with farmers. Even when Temple was a poor student, she had good writing skills. Being able to

write well helped advance her career. A press pass was safely tucked inside her pocket when she left.

The next time Temple showed up at Ron's feedlot, he stepped aside. He had little choice but to let in a reporter.

As time passed, some cowmen began to accept the tall, strong, hardworking Temple. They liked the way she handled cattle and learned how to work the machines by herself. And they admired the way she understood cattle.

If only Temple could understand people the same way! During graduate school, Temple got her first job. She worked for a company that designed cattle feedlots. The manager liked her top-notch work. But autism sometimes caused Temple problems.

Temple never made small talk with anyone. And at meetings, she spoke her mind too bluntly. Coworkers thought she was rude. Their hurt feelings went right over Temple's head. She herself was ruled by logic. She failed to understand other people's emotions.

One day, her manager plunked a can of deodorant on Temple's desk and told her to use it. Temple felt angry and embarrassed. But from then on, her grooming improved. Another time, the manager made Temple apologize for insulting a fellow worker. Since Temple couldn't read faces, she'd had no idea the other person was upset.

Temple was coming in every day in the same green outfit. The boss also asked his female secretary to take Temple shopping for work clothes. Temple couldn't stand to wear skirts. But she did buy attractive Western clothes—cotton shirts and slacks. Temple washed the new clothes several times to soften them so they didn't irritate her sensitive skin.

These early lessons at work woke up Temple. She knew she had to learn social skills to succeed in business. But she made up her mind to never marry or have children. Those relationships were just too complicated.

Important Mentors

Temple with her mother

The manager at Temple's first job became one of her mentors—trusted guides who gave her wise advice. Today, Temple speaks highly of the special mentors who believed in her and helped her to survive in the working world. Her mentors included her mother, her science teacher William Carlock, and various people in the livestock business. She always urges other autistic people to seek out mentors who can encourage their talents and help them learn to deal with social situations.

CHAPTER 7
A Cow's Point of View

By 1975, Temple had her master's degree. She also had her own business designing cattle handling equipment. Now, for the first time, her work was about to leap into the national spotlight.

At that time, tiny bugs called mites were infesting cattle herds all over Arizona, an infestation called scabies (say: SCAY-bees). The

Scabies mite

bugs ate their way under the skin of cattle and made them itch. Cattle suffering from scabies may rub off their hair because itching is driving them crazy. They may lose weight because they spend hours scratching instead of eating.

The only cure at the time was to dunk the

cattle in dip vats. Dip vats were big pools of bug poison, seven feet deep. The cattle had to submerge into the vats completely, up and over their head. Getting soaked was the only way to kill off every bitty mite.

Dip vats terrified cattle. On the ramps leading into the pools, the cows stopped dead in their tracks, afraid to budge because it looked like jumping off a cliff. No one understood that. When cattlemen forced them ahead, some cows flipped over and drowned.

Enter Temple. A manager of a feedlot in Arizona had read her magazine articles. He asked Temple to design a dip vat that cattle could enter without getting hurt. Her deadline? Just three weeks.

Temple didn't know anything about dip vats before then. But she had been inventing all her life. She was ready for this challenge.

First, Temple took a close look at cattle entering the dip vats. She saw that the ramps were too steep and slippery for the animals' hooves. She also realized their biggest fear was stepping over the pool rim into the deep liquid.

So Temple designed a dip vat with a concrete

ramp that had a gradual downward slope. Cleats were installed on the ramp so the cattle wouldn't slip. She ended cattle's fears of entering the pool by hiding the scary drop-off from their view. Cattle simply continued down the ramp into shallow water. Then the ground gave way beneath their feet and they calmly sank into the pool. In seconds, they rose to the top. Cattle can swim. Quickly and easily, they paddled to the other side and walked out of the dip vat.

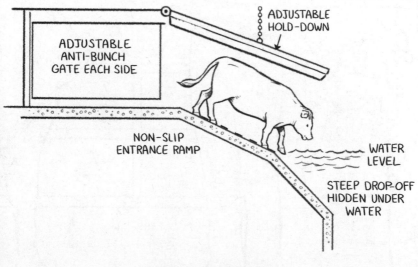

Temple's dip vat design

Temple delivered her new and improved dip vat right on time. Farmers, ranchers, and livestock handlers quickly started using it—not just in Arizona, but all over the United States!

Soon, more jobs poured in from feedlots and

packing plants. Managers hired Temple to design better, safer equipment.

Temple's approach to the jobs was unusual, just like her. She looked at problems from a "cow's-eye view." What were the animals seeing, hearing, and feeling? Once she knew that, Temple could find the right solutions.

Fear often overcame cattle in meat plants. Temple easily understood why. For two years, the cattle had been quietly raised on farms and ranches. Day after day, they had followed the same routines. Then suddenly one day they were trucked to meat plants. There they faced frightening new places and people. Temple knew that cattle are highly strung prey animals. (A prey animal is one that is hunted by other animals.) Instinct makes cows keep a constant lookout for danger so they can flee at any moment.

Temple's autism made her fearful, too. New surroundings and sudden changes threw her into a state of panic. It gave her a special window into the minds of cattle.

By looking at meat plants from a cow's viewpoint, Temple could spot problems. The plants had always been laid out in grids. Handlers herded cattle down long, straight lanes. Temple realized that straight pathways stressed cattle. Ahead in the distance, cattle could see strange people and objects—threats! The sight of them made cattle balk and freeze in their tracks.

Temple solved the problem by designing sweeping, curved lanes. Cattle ambled calmly through them, keeping their eyes on the animals directly in front of them. These winding walkways made cows feel at home. That's because in pastures, cattle naturally walk in paths that circle back home.

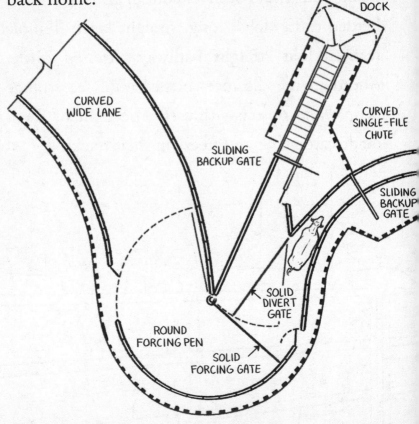

LOADING DOCK

CURVED WIDE LANE

SLIDING BACKUP GATE

CURVED SINGLE-FILE CHUTE

SLIDING BACKUP GATE

SOLID DIVERT GATE

ROUND FORCING PEN

SOLID FORCING GATE

Temple also ripped out the low, slatted fences that lined old herding lanes. Why? Because cattle are herd animals with strong instincts to stay in a group. Low fences let them see other cattle being herded in another direction. Cows bellowed loudly, wanting to join other cattle. Temple built high, solid walls so that cattle only saw the animals directly ahead of them. This kept cattle quiet and calm.

Meatpacking plants, where cattle are killed for food, posed special challenges. Federal laws were in place to make sure the animals' deaths were swift and painless. Temple made sure their deaths were also gentle and peaceful. She designed a system to carry cattle calmly through their last moments of life. Temple called it "the stairway to heaven," after a rock song by the band Led Zeppelin.

PALPATION GATE

SQUEEZE CHUTE

Here is how it worked. Cattle walked single file up a curved ramp in a packing house. Near the top, a conveyor belt slipped under the cow's belly and gently carried it forward. The ground below its hooves slipped away. The cow stayed calm and comfortable. Death would come suddenly from a fatal bolt to the head. The cattle died without fear.

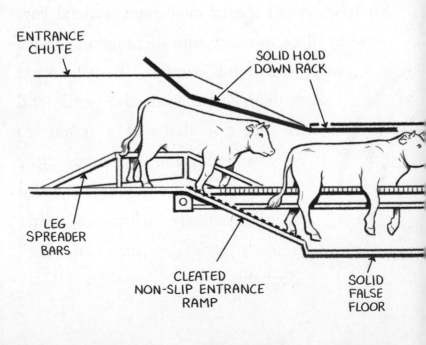

ENTRANCE CHUTE

SOLID HOLD DOWN RACK

LEG SPREADER BARS

CLEATED NON-SLIP ENTRANCE RAMP

SOLID FALSE FLOOR

Being a designer meant Temple had to draw finely detailed blueprints. Her art skills came in handy. It thrilled her to watch builders turn her drawings into steel and concrete. Just as she did on her aunt's farm, Temple pitched in and helped out, even hauling steel parts.

Today, half the cattle in the United States and Canada are handled in places Temple designed!

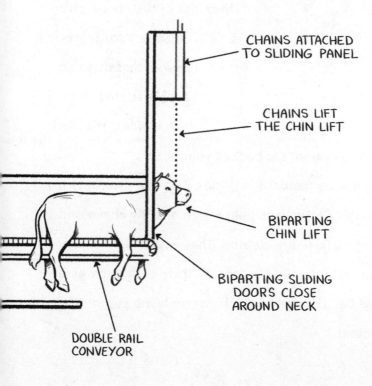

CHAINS ATTACHED TO SLIDING PANEL

CHAINS LIFT THE CHIN LIFT

BIPARTING CHIN LIFT

BIPARTING SLIDING DOORS CLOSE AROUND NECK

DOUBLE RAIL CONVEYOR

How Prey Animals See

Prey animals include cattle, deer, and buffalo. In the natural world, they survive by fleeing from their predators (attack animals). Landscape vision (also called panoramic vision) helps them stay safe. Eyes on the sides of their head give them a 360-degree view so that they can spot predators from all sides. It's like having eyes on the back of your head!

Having landscape vision has its drawbacks, though. Cattle have poor vision directly ahead and they can't judge depths. That explains why they balk at unfamiliar things in their path such as a puddle, a strange vehicle, or a plastic cup on the ground.

CHAPTER 8
Sweeping Changes

No matter how successful she became, Temple was still autistic. Understanding people still came hard for her. She has said it's like trying to survive in the "social jungle."

But little by little, Temple learned to manage her autism. Instead of shrinking from touch, she made herself shake hands. (Today her handshake is firm and confident.) She trained herself to

make eye contact while talking to people. And she taught herself basic social skills by memorizing the words and actions of others.

At home, she still relaxed in her squeeze machine. And she stayed in close contact with her mother through phone calls and letters. In time, Temple made friends who shared her interests.

Meanwhile, Temple's fame kept growing. And plant managers started calling her in to solve other puzzling problems.

One plant manager was ready to tear down an entire part of his plant because cattle refused to walk through it. Before taking that step, he asked Temple to come take a look. She showed up dressed for nitty-gritty work in a denim shirt, jeans, and boots. Throwing a long leg over the fence, Temple climbed into the corral to see what the cows saw. She spotted the problem in a flash. A flag overhead flapped in the wind. It cast waving dark shadows on the ground that looked like dangerous black pits to the cattle.

"Move the flag," Temple told the surprised manager. Problem solved.

Training cattle handlers became a big part of Temple's job. She taught them to protect cows by removing threats. A chain swinging from a ceiling, a jacket draped over a fence, a plastic water bottle that shimmers on the ground, a sparkling mud puddle, wavy glare from a sunny window, the hiss of an engine—all these things can spook cattle.

Temple also urged handlers to dump the "hot stick"—the electric prod. This gave an electric shock to animals and got them moving. Shaking plastic strips or garbage bags got herds moving just as well and didn't cause any pain.

Electric prod

Over time, Temple made the public aware of the need to protect livestock. The industry gradually changed. In the late 1990s, it was about to take a huge leap forward. And Temple led the charge.

The United States government's Department

of Agriculture hired Temple in 1996 to tour twenty-two big meatpacking plants. Her job was to inspect how well animals were treated. The cruelty she saw  horrified Temple. Two of the companies did not even obey anti-cruelty laws about swift and painless killing. Cattle in these places suffered terribly. Temple failed seven of the ten companies.

Her study became the basis of a new animal welfare standard for the industry. Animal welfare groups put pressure on fast-food restaurants. They urged them to stop buying meat from bad plants. The giant chains McDonald's, Burger King, and Wendy's turned to Temple for advice.

Temple brought the fast-food executives to see the animals for themselves. Most company chiefs had never set foot inside a slaughterhouse, even though their restaurants sold billions of hamburgers a year. On Temple's tours, they saw alarmed animals and cruelty up close. It convinced them that big meatpacking plants had to make big changes.

Executives at McDonald's and Wendy's agreed to having every one of their meat suppliers inspected. They asked Temple to draw up guide rules and train inspectors on what problems to look for. Temple created a scoring system with clear simple guidelines. *How many cows moo?* (Cows only moo when something is wrong.) Temple's guidelines permitted only three out of one hundred cattle to moo

How many cows moo?

_____

How many animals fall?

_____

How often is a stun gun used?

_____

How many run or limp?

_____

during handling. *How many animals fall? How many run or limp? How often is a stun gun used?*

The fast-food giants refused to buy meat from suppliers who flunked the test. Overnight, huge changes swept the livestock industry. Temple saw more change in six months than she had in twenty years!

Michael Chabot, a top chief in the livestock industry, has worked with Temple for years. "Slowly but surely her ideas are becoming a way of life," he said in 1998. The old ways of using force on animals are going away.

Eating Meat . . . or Not

Vegetarians choose not to eat meat at all. They do it for their health, the environment, for religious reasons, or to keep from harming animals. Yet 95 percent of Americans eat meat, including Temple.

"If I had my druthers, people would have

VEGETARIAN

evolved to be plant-eaters so we wouldn't kill animals for food," Temple has written. "But I don't see the whole human race [becoming vegetarians] anytime soon."

So Temple works to reform the livestock industry, not destroy it. She points out that farm animals treated well can live happy and healthy lives—and that people who use animals for food owe them that.

CHAPTER 9
Temple Today

In 1986, Temple sat down to write the story of her life as an autistic person. She titled it *Emergence: Labeled Autistic*. Temple described her childhood tantrums, teenage anxiety, struggles with bullies, and pain from her highly charged senses. She described how she shrank from being touched and locked herself in an inner world.

Hope rang through the book, because Temple described coping with her autism to build an exciting career. William Carlock, her high-school science teacher and mentor, wrote the book's preface. "I watched [Temple] work with her autism, sometimes in the midst of extreme discouragement . . . and saw her come to terms with it," he wrote. "I know I've seen the human spirit at its best."

Ten years later, Temple published a second memoir, *Thinking in Pictures.* In 2006, a documentary about her life was made by the British Broadcasting Company (BBC). Its title was "The Woman Who Thinks Like a Cow." And in 2010, HBO put out a movie called *Temple Grandin*, starring Claire Danes.

The books and films thrust Temple into the spotlight as a spokesperson for autistic people. The girl who couldn't speak now gives lectures to thousands. One speech Temple gave in 2010 sums up her message: "The World Needs All Kinds of Minds." After hearing Temple's message, one boy with autism told Temple, "Thank you for showing my brain isn't broken. It's just different."

Temple gives her speech titled "The World Needs All Kinds of Minds"

Temple urges autistic children to focus on their talents and interests, not on what they lack. She tells them that making friends is a lot easier when they join school clubs that center on activities they love and can share with others.

Today, Temple's life is a whirlwind of work and worldwide travel. She divides her time among three things: working for food animals, speaking out for autistic people, and teaching animal behavior at Colorado State University, where she

is a professor. Temple has also published hundreds of scientific papers and many books.

Honors and praise come Temple's way from many quarters. The *New York Times*, *The New Yorker*, National Public Radio, and *20/20* have featured articles and programs about her. And, in 2010, *Time* magazine honored her among "The 100 Most Influential People in the World."

Temple lives in Fort Collins, Colorado, not far from the university where she teaches. Her work gives her life meaning and happiness.

When she has a bit of time off, Temple sometimes visits cows. She goes to a feedlot near the university, climbs into the cows' corral—and lies on the ground! The herd backs away at first. Temple stays very still. Pretty soon, the curious animals come nearer . . . and nearer . . . until their enormous heads are looming over her.

A thousand-pound cow may lick her boot. Another will sniff her hair. The cows seem to know she's a friend, not a threat. If they only knew how much they have to thank her for.

Timeline of Temple Grandin's Life

1947	Mary Temple Grandin born in Boston, Massachusetts, on August 29
1952	Learns to speak after two years in speech therapy
1961	Expelled from junior high school
1973	Employed as livestock editor for the *Arizona Farmer Ranchman*
1975	Earns graduate degree in Animal Science at Arizona State University
1978	Designs a new dip vat for cattle
1989	Earns a PhD in Animal Science from the University of Illinois at Urbana-Champaign
1996	Develops scoring systems for new meatpacking plants for the US Department of Agriculture
2010	Honored in *Time* magazine's 2010 "The 100 Most Influential People in the World"
	Gives a TED Talk titled "The World Needs All Kinds of Minds"
	A film, *Temple Grandin*, starring Claire Danes, is released by HBO
2016	Inducted into the American Academy of Arts & Sciences
2017	Inducted into the National Women's Hall of Fame

Timeline of the World

1941 — US enters World War II after the bombing of Pearl Harbor

1943 — The term "autism" is first used by Dr. Leo Kanner in Baltimore, Maryland

1948 — Hampshire Country School is founded

1955 — Jonas Salk introduces the first polio vaccine

1958 — President Eisenhower signs the federal Humane Slaughter Act

1964 — The Beatles perform live for the first time in the United States on *The Ed Sullivan Show*

— Helen Keller receives the Presidential Medal of Freedom for her work with disabled people

1966 — The United States begins huge-scale factory farming

1969 — McDonald's, one of the first fast-food chains, sells its five billionth hamburger, fourteen years after opening its first restaurant

1974 — President Richard M. Nixon resigns after the Watergate scandal

1986 — The *Challenger* space shuttle explodes almost right after takeoff

1996 — A sheep named Dolly is the first adult mammal to be cloned

2006 — Pluto is demoted to dwarf planet status

2015 — The US Supreme Court allows same-sex marriage in all states

Bibliography

*Books for young readers

Grandin, Temple. "The World Needs All Kinds of Minds." **TED Talks**, February 2010. https://www.ted.com/talks/temple_grandin_ the_world_needs_all_kinds_of_minds.

Grandin, Temple. *Thinking in Pictures: My Life with Autism. 2nd ed.* Vintage Books: New York, 2006.

Grandin, Temple, and Catherine Johnson. *Animals in Translation: Using the Mysteries of Autism to Decode Animal Behavior.* Simon & Schuster: New York, 2005.

Grandin, Temple, and Catherine Johnson. *Animals Make Us Human: Creating the Best Life for Animals.* Mariner Books: New York, 2010.

Grandin, Temple, and Richard Panek. *The Autistic Brain: Thinking Across the Spectrum.* Mariner Books: New York, 2013.

Grandin, Temple, and Margaret Scariano. *Emergence: Labeled Autistic.* Grand Central Publishing: New York, 1986.

Jackson, Mick, director. *Temple Grandin.* HBO Films, 2010.

*Montgomery, Sy. *Temple Grandin: How the Girl Who Loved Cows Embraced Autism and Changed the World.* New York: Houghton Mifflin Harcourt, 2012.

Sacks, Oliver. "An Anthropologist on Mars." *The New Yorker.* December 27, 1993, pp. 106–125.

Sutton, Emma, director. *The Woman Who Thinks Like a Cow*. BBC
   Horizon Films, 2006.

Websites

www.templegrandin.com
www.grandin.com